THE SLIDING BOAT OUR BODIES MADE

D1571785

Also by Jennifer Barber:

Rigging the Wind
Given Away
Works on Paper

The Sliding Boat
Our Bodies Made

Jennifer Barber

THE WORD WORKS

The Word Works
P.O. Box 42164
Washington, D.C. 20015
editor@wordworksbooks.org
Cover design: Susan Pearce Design
Author photograph: Joanna Eldredge Morrissey
Cover art: Peter Brown

ISBN: 978-1-944585-55-6
LCCN: 2022931884

Acknowledgments

Thanks are due to the following publications in which these poems first appeared, sometimes in slightly different form.

Broadsided Press: "Daughter"

Charles River Journal: "Continuum"

Consequence: "The lamp in the borrowed room," "Six Weeks Left," "Buckow," "What was it like walking in the German woods, he asks"

December: "Mourner"

Dogwood: A Journal of Poetry and Prose: "In Class"

Harvard Divinity Bulletin: "At the End of July," "Ezekiel" (now "A Thousand Keys")

Ibbetson Street: "Neither Early or Late" (now "Hill Town"), "In Jerusalem," "A Still Life at the Prado," "On This Day"

Muddy River Review: "The Dream of Smoking in Bed," "The Rules Today," "Aubade," "To a Seedpod"

North American Review: "Prayers, Ourense, 1490"

Paris Review: "Pregnancy Dream" and "To My Book"

Poetry: "About My Death"

Poetry Porch: "August in Ashfield," "When I Was Able to Look," "Surgery," "No, It Is Not Too Soon"

Ruminate: "Frequency and Pitch"

The Red Letters: "Lake Constance"

Tiferet: "Mountain Outside Grenoble" (2019 Poetry Prize)

Upstreet: "When I Heard You Were Gone," "In a Gazebo, Looking Out"

Dostoyevsky Wannabee's Cities Anthology Series: Boston: "Elegy," "Overdose"

I am grateful to the MacDowell Colony and the Virginia Center for the Creative Arts. Profound thanks to Peter Brown, C.D. Collins, Linda Cutting, David Ferry, Jessica Greenbaum, George Kalogeris, Fred Marchant, Afaa M. Weaver, Leslie Williams, and to Nancy White and The Word Works team.

Contents

4

For Pete, Jeff, and Zoë

With pulsing radiance the sun rose over the horizon. The gusts continued for a while, and then it was suddenly quiet.

—W. G. Sebald, *The Rings of Saturn*, tr. Michael Hulse

Six Weeks Left

Of winter. Of summer.
Of Ellen's chemo. Of my stay

at Buckow Lake, east of Berlin.
Thirty years after the Wall fell,

the sun comes out, dappling the water,
ripening apples on the trees

behind a missing house.
The slow green surface of the lake

is the same green as the leaves
of the walnut, as the maple's wings

clustered on a branch before
a few go spiraling down.

No one's being watched
though watchfulness remains.

Elegy

The air around you, a silky skein
of blue and yellow thread.

Things giving way to other things,
the passing cars, the trees,

the skin of their leaves as thin
as eyelids letting sunlight through.

You walk into the heat of afternoon.
The houses watch you go.

You *are* the afternoon,
nowhere and everywhere.

No one can hear you when you say,
Everyone was once summer's child.

The lamp in the borrowed room

has a white shade and a gray base
with milky blossoms

down the front in a single spray,
almost Japanese,

each flower made of three
round petals, three arching stamens.

Among the blossoms are
plump white dots meant to be buds.

The lamp casts a soft light
across the night table

and the open newspaper.
The Syrian ceasefire failed again.

The Red Cross buses came too late.
There are, I know,

many hells outside this room.
A floorboard creaks

when I walk from the bed
to the fraying armchair and back.

End of June

High in the spruce, the baby
hawk that shrilled all day

is silent, the moon almost full.
Sheathed in shadow, the night climbs

the doors of the houses on our block.
The children are asleep inside.

My hand on the radio dial
lowers the news to mumbling.

Across the street, a dog's barking
sounds more and more like a question.

Lake Constance

Sunlight in the water streaming from
        my arms, the bubbles of my mouth.

No one else around. "I'm here
        between the heavens and you,

the edge of sky and the tops of trees,"
        an angel says, "between

the burning world and flooded world,
        the first day and the last,"

and his words take on the sound
        of waves mumbling onshore,

July drought mixed with August rain,
        patches of blue among the clouds

falling to the water like dropped leaves,
        their shadows gliding over fish,

breathing through them, into them.
        No: not an angel, not the words,

but the lake cradling my limbs
        in ripples striated with light.

Continuum

A split screen showed my father and me,
one of those conversations with no

content apart from the usual checking in.
"They gave me sixteen minutes," he said,

"to make this call"; then I understood
he needed permission where he was.

He wore a baggy sweater and loose slacks.
The room around him, white,

a white paper lantern overhead,
walls, window, and desk but no door.

Sure, it was a dream; even so
he put down the phone so soundlessly.

August in Ashfield

A rudimentary bird
            dents the air with a single note.

                  Doubled in the lake, the pines
                        are pointing their crowns

at the darker water in the middle,
            colder, farther from the earth,

                  like the Leopardi poem
                        I've read a hundred times

where a deep quiet
            replaces the pulse,

                  allowing your light
                        through a breach in the afternoon.

Then you're gone, a gust
            scattering needles at my feet.

The Rules Today

No trees. Nothing about death.
Or something about trees, but not death,

one with spade-shaped leaves,
one with leaves like fingers spread.

With the *Guide* I bought, I thought I'd know
a gray from a paper birch,

yellow oak from mossy cup,
comparing the acorns in my hands.

Instead I'm losing my way
among boulders and knotted roots,

familiar only with the veins
engraved in a witch hazel leaf.

These Mornings

I light a candle at daybreak.

I fill a cup with my thirst

and drink it down, and reach for more.

I'm in a flannel nightgown,

a flannel bathrobe printed with red birds.

I sleep. I wake. Another indigo

fills the window of my room.

By now the trees have shed their leaves.

I light the grapefruit-scented candle

with three wicks; I fall in love with it

and scissors and pens and paperclips.

I strip to a shadow of myself

and fill the shadow with

powders, pink and blue,

and spread them evenly across.

What I feel I feel for all of us—

the highway driver, the insomniac,

my friend waiting to hear what the doctor found.

A Thousand Keys

After the fall of Jerusalem,
in the verse where Ezekiel
is transported
to the Valley of Remains,

God whispers how
the dry bones will stand
as flesh and sinews cover them,
the breath returning.

What word would you use
for the sound of the bones?

The clatter of flint on slate?
A thousand keys
in a thousand locks?
A stack of trembling plates?

If you have a word,
do you have a word
for learning someone you love
won't be here for long?

2

Untitled

These lines have been scrubbed
of trees. Of their leaves.

Of a lamp glowing
in the hour before dawn.

Of prayers and pleas,
rain in the cupboard, snow

a future I can't touch.
Where are the trees going,

what else will be erased?
My anguish? My joy? My store

of days like these—
the only days I know.

When the Outbreak Starts

Daydreaming of spring is not forbidden.

The air is cold but the light has changed.

The forsythia tangles like kindling.

The rosebush sprouts green thorns.

The bees emerge from a drunken sleep.

A fallen twig sprawls in the sun.

The sidewalk longs for thin-soled shoes.

At the curb, two girls—I don't know whose—

look both ways, then race across.

Pregnancy Dream

At first puzzlement, then joy.

My baby-in-the-making—surely my last—
would, like a ferry heading for a wharf,
know what to do along the way.

The multiplying cells, the chemistry
of contentment spreading through my blood:

I was as ready for her birth
as I'd ever been in my childbearing years.

The natural laws stood apart
like trees onshore.

Feast

I watch a Cooper's hawk
　　　　　on a fence post, watching

sparrows crowd the juniper,
　　　　　dozens coming and going,

chattering, loud, oblivious.
　　　　　Which one will he take?

Each day a pour of days,
　　　　　each night a raft of nights.

Venus glitters in the dark.
　　　　　April consumes December.

A shadow of the moon
　　　　　waits over the street.

In Jerusalem

I trip and scrape my knee
on a cobblestone,
leaving a trace of blood on the curb.

*

In a packed café,
I'm mumbling
a warning to myself.

*

The stabbings are elsewhere.
The stabbings are in another
part of the city where I am not.

*

So many folded prayers
are wedged in the city's throat,
it's impossible to pull them out.

*

Come into my shop, he says,
come look at the necklaces,
the rings.

*

How long
have I been the enemy?
What god am I counting on?

*

A hundred times a day I touch
the passport in my pocketbook
to make sure my hand's still there.

When I Heard

Somehow I was in a car
                but also on the sidewalk
                                where several of us gathered,

milling around in our shock.
                Your wife stared at me
                                as if your death were my fault,

as if my friendship with you
                caused your heart to fail.
                        Though I loved him I never…

I wanted to explain
                in the midst of my grief
                                but the words I said were,

"Let me *speak!* Let me…"
                when the sound
                                of my own voice woke me.

From the Sidewalk

The neighbor's

cedars rise so tall

my gaze

travels up,

losing its way

among the needles

soft as feathers,

tiny spines

soaked in air,

as if I were

lying on my back

on a mountain

halfway across

the world,

taking in the trees

before me—

You famous

cedars of Lebanon!—

praising these

in the name of those.

Audubon Calendar: June

So rosy the air,
so perfect the plover,

I can't bear
to lift the page

though July and August
are also gone.

He stands on long legs
at the day's edge

in sugary sand,
his body the size of a chick,

wings tucked
against his puffy sides.

A compact beak
the color of bronze.

The round eye scanning.
If he blinks, the blink

is infinitesimal—
thinnest splinter in time.

Daughter

I've lost the notebook you filled
before you could write the alphabet,

page after page of cuneiform,

the marks you made, so dark
they dented the paper's weave.

Why think of it now? You are

heading out to your boyfriend's place,
shoulder bag packed tight,

umbrella, hairbrush, underwear.

I remember you learning to stand
alone in the middle of the floor,

watching dust motes float and spark.

You stood at the center of the world
in your overalls and round white shoes.

In Class

The other students looked up to him

> *I dream of crossing great plains with blistered feet*
> *or quiet steps on cold linoleum*

I thought he'd stopped using; his gaze was clear

> *I've been chased by devils four years now*
> *mistakes were made but I do not know how*

A big, gentle, offbeat guy

> *diseased skin flakes and falls*
> *my husk peeling like old wallpaper*

If we had talked more, one on one

> *scraped clean by prying eyes and judging teeth*

I collected their journals at semester's end

> *what a fate it is*
> *to die by one's own negligence*

> *I am nearly transparent by now*

Overdose

Two small boys wading with a net
shout to their mother,

"There's a hole! The fish got away!"

Blue spruce, green dragonfly, the trick
of pretending not to know

what happened to Jake, my student.

The sun bypasses a cloud.
Three mallards slide into the shadows.

The lake keeps lapping at the dock.

The mother tells her boys to come on out.

"No, we can't come out, not now!"

Mesopotamian Myth

—Clay Tablet III

We heard thunder, battering wind.

A giant cloud swallowed the trees.

Darkness swallowed our lanes and roofs.

Everything there was […]

[…] in the total dark.

The flood roared like a bull.

No sun, no moon, no stars. Day after day

The water rose around us till the ark

Floated and spun. I couldn't steer.

We saw the bodies of the drowned,

Their once bright faces blurred.

As for us, how are we to live

In a house of bereavement? How long?

Let daylight return. Let the sun

Light the crests of grasses, the crowns of weeds.

Let the gods regret what they have done.

3

Frequency and Pitch

In a piece on the radio
about the club-winged manakins

in a cloud forest on the Andes' slopes,
the male makes a strange music.

One feather has seven ridges;
the hard, curved tip of another

strikes the ridges like a spoon
against a washboard, hitting each ridge twice,

14 times per shake. He shakes
100 times a second—1400 notes.

The female thrills to the pulse.
Darwin said the manakins evolved

solid bones to bear the rattling.
Their flying suffered. Their music soared.

                    **

Restless after you go out,
thumbing through *World Poetry*, I find

the Cycle of the Goddess Inanna:
I bathed for the shepherd Dumuzi,

I perfumed my sides with ointment,
I coated my mouth with sweet-smelling amber,

I painted my eyes with kohl.
He shaped my loins with his fair hands,

the shepherd Dumuzi
filled my lap with cream and milk.

The oak shakes its leaves
a few at a time, then all at once

in the window by the bed.
I think of the sliding boat our bodies made.

Nasturtiums

They aren't poppies: they never
wanted to stand in
for the blood of the battlefield.

Letting the August rain
into their rambling stems,

they multiply but leave
fullness to the dahlias,
staunchness to the marigolds.

Combed by the wind,
spreading pathlessly,
they know the fondling bees.

Of the ground, near the ground,
they savor their last days.

Where Morning

The birds wake first, an hour before dawn.
       The moon thins. The watchman calls,
              Lovers and thieves,
                    the new day is here!

I slide out of bed, you still fast asleep,
       tangled in the sheet,
              a pillow in your arms.

Gathering my panties from the floor,
       I walk with the rolling slowness of a bear,
              singing,
                  The new day is here!

To a Seedpod: Questionnaire

Do you prefer a hard bed or soft?

I sleep night and day in the grass.

What is your best feature?

I'm covered with pale fur,
silky as a cat's ear.

What motto can you share with us?

Return, return
to the ground of your soul.

Which tree let go of you?

The northern magnolia.

Why do you call her northern?

She drops her leaves in fall.

Where can I find others of you?

In the Jewish graveyard.
In the field across the road.

The Mourner

I found six tea lights in a drawer
and lit them all with a single match.

*

The apples on the table
glowed like lamps.

*

I tried to hear the timbre
of my father's voice.

*

I thought of the creatures Ezekiel saw,
half-human, half-animal,
eyes all over their bodies, even their backs.

*

I couldn't weep, so I didn't.
Sometimes I cried out in my sleep.

*

Each curling wick sizzled.
Wax pooled around each flame.

Dream of Smoking in Bed

Taking a deep drag, a slow exhale.

Abandoning *Spinoza* for *The Long Goodbye*.

Dozing, burning to hear

the nearness of your step.

Scorching a hole in the sheet,

the damage done, the flames.

Later, before dawn,

we pass a cigarette back and forth,

licking the ash on our lips.

Orders Concerning the Jews

—Toledo Court, 1412

"None may hold office.
None may change their names.

"None shall be a spice seller or chemist
or physician to any of our faith.

"None shall be addressed
with the title Don or Doña.

"The women must wear full-length shawls.
Ornaments in gold are not allowed.

"The men must grow beards and wear their hair uncut
as they did in the days of Christ.

"Thus it will be clear
at a glance who they are."

On This Day

A light goes on in the house
at the top of the hill, behind the school.

A car alarm at dawn, no thief in sight.
A tree rubs a cloud between its fingers.

What good is noticing such things
when you're furious with me?

To say nothing of the squirrel
upside down, acrobatic on the trunk.

Remnants of snow dissolve
from the ground like a wrong idea.

*

A splinter in the meat of my palm
won't surface, despite the probing needle.

I got it running my hand along
the railing as I climbed the attic stairs

to sit and read at my desk.
No book on the shelf spoke to me.

Love wrecks us, doesn't it?
Love throws us a life rope.

*

Oak branches toss shade
onto the curtain in the den.

A driver takes a package from his truck.
Angels, unlike cherubim,

appear sometimes without their wings
in the guise of a messenger.

Not a vision of another world:
a squinting toward what disappears.

Cherubim carry the scroll of days.
Angels say the words.

Prayers, Pontevedra

—Ysaq Vello, 1490

Long days. Longer nights.
The wet wind. The dry wind.

Dust across the sill.

Neighbors who don't speak.
The failure of my prayers.

The advent of harsh laws.

Dust across the sill.
The wet wind. The dry wind.

Long days. Longer nights.

A Still Life at the Prado

No way to pierce the lemon
or split these grapes that swell
against their purple skins.

The fish with jeweled viscera
spills on a plate. The bread
cools in its ochre crust.

A thin black line in the eye
of the pheasant cracks
across your retina: you are

this moment trespassing
layers of the visible
to watch the painter's hands

arrange three oranges.
They glow like coals in you
before you disappear.

Last Day in Zamora

—Judah Pérez, 1492

Before the Edict,

before I sold my vineyard,
already in bloom,

our scholars proved
our ancestors were *here*

in Castillia y León

and not responsible for
the death of Jesus in Judaea.

In the monarchs' view
and in the eyes of the court,

a worthless argument.

Tomorrow we'll leave
our houses, our streets,

the graveyard holding our dead.

Boston in December

Hard snow on the ground.
          The year closing down.

           Night so fast the eye
                darkens like a lake.

The new moon
          hones its blade.

          I've read tears are stored
                in the part of the eye

called the lacrimal lake.
          Before they are tears.

From a Gazebo, Looking Out

The morning sky is bright.
I've lit
three candles I found on the table.

Water shimmers near the dock.

Each window has a band
of colored glass:
the emerald
turns the viburnum leaves a darker green.

Anything can happen, Horace said.
A falling tree can kill you.
A heart can fail.

I left my husband
sleeping in the house,
his raspy breathing getting through.

A hooded crow arrives
with a thump on the gazebo roof.

Wind pours silver across the lake.

A call somewhere
among the trees
warns and warns again: anything.

4

Aubade

Because mourning doves believe
        aubades are about them,
                opening their beaks to blend
           sorrow with a hazy joy

as when the dawn
        grows audible,
                rain tapering off
                    through the dripping trees,

you and I are listening in bed,
        neither fated to
                have lost the other yet.
           Albada in Spanish,

a song of greeting
        or of parting at daybreak,
                propagation of light
                    across our floor.

About My Death

I don't want to see it coming
like late summer roses waiting to bloom

or a highway I remember in Spain,
a giant black cut-out bull

as a hilltop billboard.
Instead let me be half asleep,

the Never and Forever twins,
one in a brown dress, one in blue,

steeped in the shadows of my room,
the air replacing my breath

with flow and husk, and then the sound.
Let me leave each twin a gift:

a milky quartz on the night table,
my worn gold wedding ring.

Cezanne's "Flowers and Fruit"

A glass pitcher filled
with daisies and anemones
holds down one end of a white cloth.

The other end bunches
under fruit that looks like it might roll:
a green pear and a yellow.

Even the table seems to buck
as if it were on a ship.

Steadying yourself, you see
traces of blue in the cloth,
a coolness under the ripe flesh.

Your hand moves to touch
the green pear, the yellow
in the summer they exhale.

Holbein's "Christ Lying in the Grave"

You see into the coffin
as though a panel had been replaced
by glass. How thin he is,

a red gash beneath his ribs,
his head and his feet tinged green.

How near the coffin lid to his face.
How near the surface your own fear
of tight spaces, how hard to breathe.

You notice his hand,
dark green, and below the wrist,
a purple bruise where the nail goes in.

That he will return
to his disciples walking the road
is nowhere foretold here

unless you consider the air
lit by a hidden candle.

Hill Town

You're walking along a road that climbs
past a farmhouse, a field, another farm.

No cars or trucks in driveways; nobody's home
so you can choose the house you want,

this one, a patch of Queen Anne's lace
and two off-white horses in the yard,

broad of back but plowless, wagonless.
A yellow cat steps past you into the long grass.

Your mouth opens as you eavesdrop on the trees
in the wind's throat, their dry fricatives.

Will a dog appear, barking like a fiend?
If he does, don't listen. Don't forget you are

traveler and lookout, prodigal,
each turn in the road a place to leave.

When I Was Able to Look

Behind the first door I saw
           a tricycle at the curb.

Behind the second door
           stars dropped like fireflies.

At the third I beheld
           an infant wailing in my arms.

The fourth door opened to
           a mule turning a mill stone.

I came to the fifth door
           down a hallway of sloped walls.

At the sixth I unclasped
           my necklace of clay beads.

At the seventh door
           I removed my shoes.

Surgery

After the rain,
the white hydrangea
cascades
into bloom.

Though you're home,
I thirst for you.

A few petals
on the ground
look up dazed
at the new leaves.

No, It Is Not Too Soon

Sunlight scatters topaz on the lake

past the end of the dock,

tall splashes of light

that stretch their necks like swans.

A boulder lifts its shoulders

through oval gray shadows.

A hummingbird on the laundry line:

a clothespin come to life.

If only you'd emerge

naked from the little house,

abandoning your book,

we could wade into each other again.

Duration

Rain drowning the shriveled marigolds.
The way this month seems like six.

The goddess Inanna
searching for her husband, Dumuzi,

after her escape from the Underworld.
She doesn't know that demons

captured him to punish her.
They strike him with a shepherd's crook.

She doesn't know that demons
pierce his cheek with a nail.

They shatter his cup and splinter his churn.
They seize his goats and sheep.

They strip him of scepter and crown.
Inanna searches on and on.

At last a gossiping fly leads her to
the barren steppe where Dumuzi lies.

He must spend half of every year
beside the Queen of the World Below.

Dumuzi weeps. Inanna weeps.
Inanna and Dumuzi weep.

Even the word duration is hard.
As waiting is. As seasons are.

There are bridges elsewhere over a river,
terrasses and market stalls,

but here this morning, the first snow
adheres to autumn leaves

clinging to branches. The trees lean
forward with the unaccustomed weight.

Mountain Outside Grenoble

What I remember most
is a confusion of bells,
sheep like woolen slipknots
over the tufted grass.

The din of dogs
warned us off
as if we'd come to abscond
with a lamb in our arms.

Hundreds of feet below,
the city lay in a haze
of cars, buses, and heat.

Where the trail
went under trees,
we heard the cuckoos' cries,
contrapuntal, invisible.

Let me pour it all again
into the cup of my ear,
the bells, the cuckoos'
call and response.

However far away,
let me keep this place
among my gathering flock.

Foothills, Memorial

I've forgotten the names
        cut into the granite

in Seyssinet-Pariset
        where the road rises

toward the plateau of Vercors
        but I remember learning

the Resistance fighters
        captured and held there

were executed facing the cliff
        in 1944, just before

the end of the Occupation.
        Our friend was silent

next to us. We'd walked
        a grassy path to get there.

We stood reading but not
        remembering the names.

What was it like walking
in the German woods, he asks

No guard tower or remnant of a wall.
A stinging nettle brushed my knee.

Pinecones broke with a crackle underfoot,
the whole grove dry as kindling.

The bark looked reddish in the copper light.
After the pines, a stand of beech

with their smooth limbs, their rustling as if
the woods had only ever known shade.

To My Book

I've been grooming you for years.
           Now I'm asking you to go

through the gate unafraid
           past the weeds towering

in the heat at the end of July,
           the sun dropping like a red

bucket into a well of clouds.
           You look like no one I know

and everyone I've known,
           the branches of the specimen elm

reaching their furthest shape,
           a wind rustling at the door

of the cottage beyond the field
           whose sleeper breathes the same

evening. Lie down, my book:
           lie down beside the sleeper.

Buckow

By evening the lake is a darker green
around the rim of itself.

A moss green, I want to say,
but moss has nothing to do with the tall

grasses in the shallows by the shore,
some with their pennant leaves blown back

by the rising breeze, others gleaming
like the blade-edge of a sword.

                    *

Evening, yes—even the word bends.
Other parts of the lake are gray—

colorless, as if seen through glass.
A duck floats with her glittering

wake, her slow trajectory.
Brecht in Buckow, toward the end of his life,

eight years since the end of the war,
said he wanted to see with younger eyes

the pine trees' copper light. He wrote,
The great Carthage started three wars.

After the first, she was still prosperous.
After the second, she was still livable.

After the third, she was nowhere to be found…
Here beyond the dock, beyond

the lily pads like footsteps, the lake
glows like silver paper under a cloud.

Notes

p. 11: "August in Ashfield": the Leopardi poem referred to is "L'infinito." The translation I read, by Robert Bringhurst, includes the lines "…about the deep quiet/that happens sometimes in the heart and that almost/replaces the pulse."

pp. 27 and 28: "In Class" and "Overdose": these poems are in memory of Jacob Haseltine, 1997-2017. The italicized lines in "In Class" are from his class journal.

p. 29: "Mesopotamian Myth": this poem invents new lines and also adapts some lines from the volume *Myths from Mesopotamia: Creation, the Flood, Gilgamesh, and Others*, edited and translated by Stephanie Dalley.

pp. 33-34: "Frequency and Pitch": the quoted lines are from the Akkadian "Cycle of Inanna," translated by Diane Wolkstein and Samuel Noah Kramer, in the volume *World Poetry*.

pp. 40, 43, 45: The background for these poems comes from *Los judíos en Galicia* (1044-1492) by María Gloria de Antonio Rubio and *Los judíos de Zamora: Una cronología anotada* by Jesús Jambrina. The speakers and the words in "Prayers, Pontevedra" and "Last Day in Zamora" are invented.

p. 44: "A Still Life at the Prado": the still life described is a composite of paintings by Franciso Zurbarán, b. 1598, d. 1664.

p. 59: "Duration": the writing of this poem was influenced by reading "The Descent of Inanna to the Underworld" in *Inanna: Queen of Heaven and Earth*, by Diane Wolkstein and Samuel Noah Kramer.

pp. 65-66: "Buckow": the German word "Abend" means evening. The observation about the pine trees' copper light is from Bertolt Brecht's volume titled *Buckow Elegies* (1953). The sentences about Carthage were written by Brecht in 1951.

About the Author

Jennifer Barber's previous poetry collections are *Works on Paper*, recipient of the 2015 Word Works Tenth Gate Prize and published in 2016; *Given Away* (Kore Press, 2012); and *Rigging the Wind* (2003), winner of the Kore Press 2002 First Book Award. *Given Away* was translated into French by poet Emmanuel Merle and published as *Délivrances* by La Rumeur Libre in 2018. She founded the literary journal *Salamander* in 1992 and served as its editor in chief at Suffolk University in Boston through 2018. Recent poems have appeared in *Consequence*, *Broadsided*, *December*, the *Harvard Divinity Bulletin*, *Paris Review*, *Poetry*, *Tiferet* (2019 Poetry Prize), and elsewhere. She has received fellowships from the MacDowell Colony and the Virginia Center for the Creative Arts and is the current poet laureate of Brookline, MA.

About the Artist

Peter Brown is an artist, writer, and translator. With co-translators Caroline Talpe and Emmanuel Merle, he has published two books of poetry in French translation: the poems of David Ferry, *Qui est là?* (La Rumeur Libre, 2018) and the poems of Arthur Gold, *14 Poèmes (Une Période de Maladie)*, (Éditions Encre & lumière, 2021). *Elsewhere on Earth* (Guernica Editions), an English translation of poems by Emmanuel Merle, appeared in 2014. Brown's collection of short stories, *A Bright Soothing Noise* (UNT Press, 2010), won the Katherine Anne Porter Prize.

About The Word Works

Since its founding in 1974, The Word Works has steadily published volumes of contemporary poetry and presented public programs. Its imprints include The Washington Prize, The Tenth Gate Prize, The Hilary Tham Capital Collection, and International Editions.

Monthly, The Word Works offers free literary programs in its Café Muse and Poets vs The Pandemic series, and each summer it holds free poetry programs in its Joaquin Miller Poetry Series which also presents two high school winners of the Jacklyn Potter Young Poets Competition. Word Works programs have included "In the Shadow of the Capitol," a symposium and archival project on the African American intellectual community in segregated Washington, D.C.; the Gunston Arts Center Poetry Series; the Poet Editor panel discussions at The Writer's Center; Master Class workshops; and a writing retreat in Tuscany, Italy.

As a 501(c)3 organization, The Word Works has received awards from the National Endowment for the Arts, the National Endowment for the Humanities, the D.C. Commission on the Arts & Humanities, the Witter Bynner Foundation, Poets & Writers, The Writer's Center, Bell Atlantic, the David G. Taft Foundation, and others, including many generous private patrons.

An archive of artistic and administrative materials in the Washington Writing Archive is housed in the George Washington University Gelman Library. The Word Works is a member of the Community of Literary Magazines and Presses and its books are distributed by Small Press Distribution.

wordworksbooks.org

Other Word Works Books

Annik Adey-Babinski, *Okay Cool No Smoking Love Pony*
Rachel J. Bennett, *Mothers and Other Fairy Tales*
Karren L. Alenier, *Wandering on the Outside*
Karren L. Alenier, ed., *Whose Woods These Are*
Andrea Carter Brown, *September 12*
Christopher Bursk, ed., *Cool Fire*
Willa Carroll, *Nerve Chorus*
Grace Cavalieri, *Creature Comforts*
Abby Chew, *A Bear Approaches from the Sky*
Nadia Colburn, *The High Shelf*
Henry Crawford, *The Binary Planet*
Barbara Goldberg, *Berta Broadfoot and Pepin the Short*
        / *Breaking & Entering: New and Selected Poems*
Akua Lezli Hope, *Them Gone*
Frannie Lindsay, *If Mercy*
Elaine Magarrell, *The Madness of Chefs*
Chloe Martinez, *Ten Thousand Selves*
Marilyn McCabe, *Glass Factory*
JoAnne McFarland, *Identifying the Body*
Leslie McGrath, *Feminists Are Passing from Our Lives*
Kevin McLellan, *Ornitheology*
Ron Mohring, *The Boy Who Reads in the Trees*
A. Molotkov, *Future Symptoms*
Ann Pelletier, *Letter That Never*
W.T. Pfefferle, *My Coolest Shirt*
Ayaz Pirani, *Happy You Are Here*
Robert Sargent, *Aspects of a Southern Story* / *A Woman from Memphis*
Roger Smith, *Radiation Machine-Gun Funk*
Julia Story, *Spinster for Hire*
Julie Marie Wade, *Skirted*
Miles Waggener, *Superstition Freeway*
Fritz Ward, *Tsunami Diorama*
Camille-Yvette Welsch, *The Four Ugliest Children in Christendom*
Amber West, *Hen & God*
Maceo Whitaker, *Narco Farm*